Fashion

Eleanor Van Zandt

Titles in this series

Art
Cinema
Communications
Fashion
Farming
Medicine
Transport
Warfare

Editor: Francesca Motisi

Designer: Charles Harford HSD

Front cover, main picture *British Fashion Awards – Skirt and sweater by Linda Edwards for Jump (1982).*
Front cover, inset *The Hoop-la line in black silk crêpe (1957).*
Back cover *The Punk 'look' of the 1980s.*

First published in 1988 by
Wayland (Publishers) Ltd
61 Western Road, Hove
East Sussex BN3 1JD, England

© Copyright 1988 Wayland (Publishers) Ltd

British Library Cataloguing in Publication Data
Van Zandt, Eleanor
20th Century Fashion. –
(20th Century)
1. Fashion–History–20th Century–
Juvenile literature
I. Title   II. Series
746.9'2   TT504

ISBN 1–85210–127–X

Typeset by Kalligraphics Ltd, Redhill, Surrey, England
Printed by G. Canale and C.S.p.A., Turin, Italy
Bound by Casterman, S.A., Belgium

Contents

1900–1918

Fine Feathers

The twentieth century has brought enormous changes in fashion, as in every other aspect of life. Women's clothing, in particular, has been through many changes in the past ninety years. There are dozens of reasons for this, but two of the most important factors have been the changing role of women and the creation of a more equal society.

Ladies . . .

As the new century opened, the only women who could afford to be truly fashionable were 'ladies of leisure', a very small percentage of the population as a whole. These women had the time and the money to have their clothes made to measure by expert designers, or couturiers, preferably in Paris. Fashions of the time were so complicated that they could not be duplicated by mass-production methods, which were then in their infancy. Women with less money went to a local dressmaker who did her best to copy the Paris fashions, or they made their own clothes.

The fashionable lady of Edwardian times (as the years from 1901 to 1910 are called, after the reigning British king, Edward VII) was an imposing sight. Forced into the fashionable 'S-curve' shape by an undergarment incredibly called a 'health corset', she glided through a drawing room like a proud ship; bosom leading, bottom well back, her long, flared skirts trailing behind her over several rustling petticoats. For evening, her gown

Below Edwardian ladies wore elaborate hats decorated with artificial flowers or feathers.

would be low-cut, her arms bare and she would wear elegant evening gloves. In the daytime the sleeves were long and the collar up nearly to her ear lobes. Her collar would be stiffened, like her corset, by strips of whalebone, a horny substance taken from the mouths of certain types of whale.

All of her clothes, except those that were meant specifically to be worn in the country, were lavishly trimmed with braid, embroidery or lace. On top of her elaborately-dressed hair she wore an even more elaborate hat, decorated with feathers or artificial flowers and held in place with one or two fierce-looking hatpins. Depending on the weather, a muff or parasol might complete her costume.

. . . and gentlemen

Men's clothes in the early 1900s may not have been quite so uncomfortable as women's, but rules about correct dress were nevertheless fairly rigid by today's standards. London set the fashion for men, just as Paris did for women; Britain's new king, Edward VII, helped to maintain the conservative traditions of dress that had been established in the nineteenth century. The king would occasionally wear the increasingly popular lounge suit (now the normal business suit), but generally dressed in the more formal frock coat. This had a straight or slightly flared skirt reaching well down the thigh and was often double-breasted. It was made in only two colours: black or dark grey, and was worn with matching, striped or checked trousers and a top hat. The elegant morning coat – now reserved for formal daytime functions such as weddings – was at the turn of the century considered relatively informal.

For work, most professional men and executives favoured the frock coat, while the lounge suit, usually in black, was the standard uniform for middle and lower-echelon office-workers.

In Europe shirts were still generally of the 'tunic' type, which were pulled on over the head, although the American 'coat' type was becoming more popular. Both kinds of shirt were worn with a separate, stiffly starched collar and a necktie.

Formal evening wear, then as now, was the black tailcoat and trousers with white

Right King Edward VII (photographed in 1875 when Prince of Wales) wearing a top hat. The King was always impeccably but conservatively dressed.

waistcoat, shirt and bow-tie. The dinner jacket (which is also called a tuxedo in the USA) was, however, beginning to make an appearance at slightly less formal occasions.

A popular outfit for the country was the Norfolk jacket, which had first been introduced in the 1880s. This was a belted jacket, usually of tweed or checked fabric, worn with knickerbockers, woollen stockings and a cloth cap.

Improved methods of waterproofing discovered around this time led to the development of raincoats for men. One type of raincoat was specially designed to withstand the wet, muddy conditions endured by soldiers in the trenches during the First World War. Today, seventy years later, the trench coat which was originally designed for a strictly utilitarian purpose, has become a fashion classic for both women and men.

Left Edward VII dressed for shooting in a Norfolk jacket and knickerbockers.

Below A lounge suit (1903).

New silhouettes

A trend towards more practical clothes for women began in the late 1800s and continued in the early 1900s. Women were beginning to lead more active lives, taking part in sports such as golf, shooting and cycling, which required more easy-fitting garments. In the USA, the shirtwaist blouse, which was of similar design to a man's shirt, became very popular. Although it was not particularly loose-fitting, it was considerably more informal than some of the multi-layered, restrictive garments that had preceded it. In Europe, the tailor-made suit, with its simple lines and a skirt that just cleared the ground, had already been introduced for country wear. Now it began to be worn in town, especially by the growing number of working women. More loose-fitting coats were specially designed for riding in 'horseless carriages', or cars.

In 1908 the S-curve began to be replaced by a more natural, vertical silhouette. This was mainly the creation of the French designer Paul Poiret. Bosoms and hips were allowed to resume more or less normal positions, although they were still firmly encased in a corset. Skirts hung straight down to the floor, or just above it, over a single narrow petticoat. Sometimes the wearer's natural waistline would be ignored in the shaping of the garment, and an exaggeratedly high 'Empire' waistline would be used instead.

Really comfortable clothes, however, were still a long way off. Around 1910, skirts became still narrower and were known as 'hobble skirts'. As their name suggests, these garments made it impossible for the wearer to walk normally. To avoid splitting the seams, the prudent woman wore special linked garters which kept her stride in check. Closely related to the hobble skirt was the peg-top skirt, which was another ankle-length garment. This was cut very full on the hips, with a number of drapes and folds, but became a good deal narrower towards the hem.

Hats, on the other hand, became wider. They were often decorated with a mini-mountain of cabbage roses or feathers, and had to be very carefully balanced on the head. Women might have been on the verge of securing the right to vote, but they were still prisoners of their own clothing.

Right In the 1900s women's clothing became more practical to suit their increasingly active lifestyles.

Far right Emmeline Pankhurst (who launched the militant suffragette campaign in 1906) enjoys the freedom of movement a loose coat allows.

Opposite page An evening gown designed by Paul Poiret illustrating his 'lampshade' silhouette; the tunic was wired around the hem.

Birds of Paradise

When the Ballets Russes first came to Paris in 1909 they caused a sensation. It was not just their dancing and music that excited people; it was also their brilliantly coloured costumes designed by Leon Bakst. Particularly influential were those worn for *Schéhérazade*, which looked towards Persia and the East for inspiration.

In no time at all, the 'Oriental Look' – reinterpreted by Paul Poiret – became the vogue. Out went wide, heavy hats and restrained pastel colours; in came sleek satin turbans (often crowned with a feather) and vivid, glowing colours. A few daring souls even wore harem trousers. The fashionable narrow silhouette was transformed by the addition of tunics of various kinds, including Poiret's vaguely oriental, wired 'lampshade' tunic.

The 'Oriental Look' lingered on until the beginning of the First World War. Then more sober fashions began to reflect the growing awareness that the party, for the time being, was over.

Right A satin turban (1911) crowned with a feather, designed by Paul Poiret.

Below The 'Oriental Look'. A white dress (1913) with a violet embroidered tunic and matching turban.

Above Some of Paul Poiret's designs.

Left A fabric design by Raoul Dufy. Many of Poiret's gowns were made from fabrics designed by Dufy.

Paul Poiret (1879–1944)

Born in Paris, the son of a humble cloth merchant, Paul Poiret was apprenticed to an umbrella manufacturer while in his teens. He taught himself to sketch and began selling dress designs to leading French couturiers.

In 1904 Poiret opened his own fashion house. He soon became one of the most influential dress designers in the world, introducing in rapid succession, the new natural line, the hobble skirt and the 'Oriental Look'. In 1911 he launched his own perfume, 'Rosine', a move that set a trend other French designers would follow. Poiret was an enthusiastic patron of the arts and in both his work and his private life this admiration for the arts was evident. For example, he made available the funds to establish a school of textile and furniture design and many of his most striking gowns were made from fabrics designed by the famous painter Raoul Dufy.

After the First World War (during which he had closed his business), Poiret began designing again. His clothes were less popular in the 1920s however, and eventually the combination of changing taste and his carelessness with money caused him to become bankrupt.

The Jazz Age

The image we tend to associate with the 1920s – the 'flapper', with her knee-length skirts, boyish bob and giddy lifestyle – did not, in fact, appear until the middle of the decade. In any case, she was only a caricature of the true 'new woman' who emerged during and after the First World War.

The independent woman

The war had brought an unprecedented number of women into the workforce, and it had effectively left them responsible for large areas of society and the economy while men were fighting at the front. With the large numbers of young men killed during the war, women's new position was maintained after the 1918 armistice. They finally won the right to vote (although full equality on this issue did not come until 1928) and played a much fuller role than previously in society. The 'new woman' who emerged after the war had experienced independence, responsibility and in many cases, personal sorrow. It is not surprising that the clothing she wore reflected these things. The fuller, shorter skirt of 1918 – up to mid-calf level – permitted the easy stride appropriate for a working woman. But the post-war silhouette was shapeless and featured long, severely cut or baggy jackets. An intimidating wide-brimmed hat, set low on the forehead, completed the business-like look.

Left A 1923 picture of the Swedish-born actress Greta Garbo wearing the long and shapeless style of the post-war years.

Above Women wearing overalls to protect their clothes. They are working on aircraft propellers during the First World War.

Coco Chanel
(1883–1971)

Gabrielle ('Coco') Chanel expressed, in her work and in her life, the new freedom achieved by women in the twentieth century. When she launched her couture business after the First World War it was the beginning of a great success story.

Chanel made the kind of clothes that she herself liked to wear: simple, comfortable clothes that could be put on and then forgotten. At a time when dressing fashionably involved a great deal of time and effort, this was a revolutionary idea. Her easy-fitting cardigans, crisply pleated skirts and elegantly simple jersey dresses set the trends followed by other designers throughout the 1920s and by many others since then.

When, after a period of retirement, Chanel re-opened her couture house in 1954, she proved that she had lost none of her mastery of line. The classic Chanel suit, her most famous creation, dates from this period. And the ideas underlying her work created guidelines for modern fashion.

Above *The French designer Coco Chanel in 1928. Chanel's designs reflected the new-found freedom of twentieth-century women.*

Right *The 'uniform' of the late 1920s was inspired and imposed by Chanel, the first designer who made it smart not to look rich.*

Girls will be boys

After a few ups and downs in the early 1920s, skirts shot up to the knee in 1925 and stayed there for the next three years. For the first time in Western history, women's legs (the lower half of them, anyway), were on full view. Even more shockingly, ladies who would previously have refrained from wearing bright make-up were now wearing dark eye shadow and bright red lipstick giving the desired sultry look made fashionable by the 'vamps' of the movies.

Left A white organdy summer dress of the early 1920s embroidered with flowers.

Below The 'shapeless' boyish look of the 1920s included an extremely short haircut.

In most respects, however, the women of the 1920s tried to look as sexless as possible. Dresses hung straight from the shoulders, bypassing the waist. The garment's waistline was placed low, over the hips, and sometimes emphasized with a belt or sash. But the hips were expected to be slim; the boyish figure was the ideal. Women who were not naturally flat-chested wore special bust-flattening bras. The boyish effect was completed by an extremely short 'shingle' haircut and a cloche hat. A pair of dangling earrings or a rope of pearls might be the only concession to traditionally 'feminine' appearance.

Many of the styles of the 1920s had a severely geometric cut or seaming, which was probably the result of the influence of Cubist painters and of the functional architecture and furnishings of the day known as Art Deco. But some had a softer look. The designs of Madeleine Vionnet, a rival of Chanel, were beautifully cut and draped elegantly over the figure.

Towards the end of the decade there was a move towards lower hemlines. For evening, skirts might be knee-length in front and long at the back, or have a pointed handkerchief hemline.

Right A dress of the mid-1920s. The fashionable cloche hat and dangling earrings completed the outfit.

The new informality

By the end of the First World War, the frock coat had gone the way of the horse-drawn carriage, and the lounge suit was firmly established as normal daytime dress for men. Even the lounge suit was now being replaced, for informal social occasions, by a tweed sports jacket and flannel trousers. Cut narrow and tapering in the early 1920s, trouser legs became very wide – up to 60cm around – in the mid-1920s. These were known as Oxford bags. Patterned fabrics, such as checks, became acceptable for town wear. To match the wider trousers, jackets were often double-breasted and had boxy, padded shoulders.

Instead of a waistcoat, a man might wear a V-necked knitted slipover. For golf, knickerbockers – or the slightly larger plus-fours – might be worn with a long-sleeved Fair Isle pullover, a fashion set by the Prince of Wales, later Edward VIII.

The most flamboyant garment worn by men in the 1920s was the raccoon coat. Popular with American university students, this voluminous garment reached well below the knees.

Right Clothes for informal occasions became popular for both sexes.

Below The Duke of Windsor (later Edward VIII) wearing plus-fours, long-sleeved Fair Isle pullover and tweed cap. This was a fashion particularly associated with the Prince.

The necktie

The evolution of the necktie has taken place over the last 300 years, but a tie resembling those worn today did not appear until the late 1800s, when the cravat worn by Victorian men became narrower and various new ways of tying it were devised. The knot used most often today, the 'four-in-hand', is said to have taken its name from the coachmen who first adopted it. Bow ties were popular around the turn of the century and still remain an essential part of evening dress, while the elegant ascot tie is worn with morning dress.

For most of this century, when men's clothing remained basically conservative, the choice of necktie was almost the only opportunity for a man to express his individuality and his taste in colour. This might be done on a very subtle level, with the 'old school tie' or a discreet dark stripe or paisley. But in recent years more adventurous colours and patterns have gained acceptance, allowing even the most soberly suited executive to sport a little 'plumage'.

Above *The Duke of Windsor (Prince of Wales) and Crown Prince Hirohito of Japan dressed for golf. Although intended for sport these clothes became popular for informal day wear in the 1920s.*

Glamour and Hard Times

With the crash of the US stock market in 1929 and the world-wide Depression that followed, the playful mood of the 1920s vanished. Economies in nearly all parts of the world suffered, and millions of people were reduced to poverty as a result of unemployment. A new, more sober mood prevailed, bringing with it more grown-up-looking fashions.

Right The yellow dress reflects the softer look of the 1930s with a gently flaring skirt and natural waistline.

Below A slinky, trailing 1930s evening dress made of gold lamé.

A softer look

The fashionable length for skirts fell, in 1930, to just below mid-calf level and stayed there until 1939. These skirts tended to be gently flared and often featured interesting seaming and pleats or godets below the knee. The fashionable line was long and slim, but it was now acceptable to have curves, and the waistline assumed its natural position. The invention of latex yarn also helped in the creation of a smooth silhouette. Before this, corsetry had generally been stiffened with whalebone, but now a more flexible, and comfortable, alternative was available.

Evening dresses were floor-length and slinky; satin and crêpe de Chine were favourite fabrics and dresses were often backless. The 1930s also brought longer hair, especially towards the end of the decade, when it began to be worn shoulder-length or piled on to the top of the head in curls or in two sleek rolls. Only the padded shoulders introduced by Schiaparelli in 1933 ran counter to the prevailing feminine line of the period.

Above *A satin evening dress designed by Elsa Schiaparelli.*

Inset *Elsa Schiaparelli was the third most important designer in French fashion, after Chanel and Vionnet, during the inter-war period.*

Elsa Schiaparelli (1890—1973)

It is not surprising that there has in recent times been a renewal of interest in Elsa Schiaparelli, one of the most important designers of the 1930s. She had the kind of witty approach to fashion that is so popular today, and the padded shoulders she popularized have recently enjoyed a revival.

Italian by birth, Schiaparelli first began designing after moving to Paris in 1920. She started with knitwear, designing sweaters with unusual motifs, such as a fake white bow on a black background. Such visual jokes were to be a hallmark of many of her clothes. Buttons might be in the shape of lollipops or guitars; fabrics were printed with circus elephants and clowns or, in one case, with a huge lobster. Her famous hats took all kinds of strange shapes and even included one that looked like a lamb chop.

Many of her clothes, however, were elegant and sophisticated. Her beautifully embroidered evening suits and lounging pyjamas were worn by the most fashionable women of the time, including the Duchess of Windsor and many film stars. Schiaparelli loved bright colours; her favourite was a bright shade of pink which she dubbed 'shocking'.

19

Fashions under the sun

For centuries women had gone to great lengths to protect their skin from the sun, with big hats, parasols and clothes that covered them from chin to toe. This was due to the idea that grew up in the Middle Ages that a woman with white skin was a lady, probably because she did not have to work out of doors, as most women of the time did.

Then in the late 1920s and the 1930s sunbathing became fashionable. It was a special mark of status – and still is – to have a tan in the winter.

The vogue for sunbathing inspired some new fashions. The voluminous bathing costume of the past, with its skirt, stockings, long sleeves and matching hat, was replaced in the 1920s by a one-piece costume, which became progressively shorter and lower-cut with the passing years. In the 1930s the two-piece suit with bare midriff appeared. (Some evening dresses were also designed with bare midriffs.) Men abandoned suits with straps for swimming trunks.

Shorts, an American invention, became popular for both sexes, and beach pyjamas, with flared legs and bare arms, were fashionable for strolling along the promenade. Bare-backed sundresses were another new fashion of this period.

Below *This bulky 1912 taffeta swimming costume contrasts strongly with today's skimpy swimwear.*

Fashion and films

In the 1930s and 1940s the cinema reached the peak of its popularity. The movies offered an escape from the grim realities of the Depression and, later, from those of the war.

Movie stars had the kind of adoring public that pop stars have today, and like pop stars they had an enormous influence on what people wore. Of course, the clothing worn by characters in films reflected the prevailing fashions of the times; but Hollywood exerted an influence of its own.

When Clark Gable removed his shirt in *It Happened One Night* and was seen to be wearing no vest, the sale of vests plummeted all over America. Greta Garbo's pencil-thin eyebrows and slouch hat, Jean Harlow's platinum blonde hair and clinging white satin evening dresses and Joan Crawford's aggressively padded shoulders were among the looks that swept over North America and Europe. Hollywood's own dress designers, such as Edith Head and Adrian, may have looked to Paris for some of their inspiration, but it was their styles that were seen and copied by millions.

Above *The American film stars Jean Harlow and William Powell. Film stars of the 1930s and 1940s influenced the way people looked. Jean Harlow's platinum blonde hair was copied by many women.*

Dressed for war

Throughout the Second World War (1939–1945) fashion was more or less at a standstill. The German occupation of Paris resulted in the closing-down of many of the French fashion houses. Shortages of fabric and labour made rationing necessary, and with relatively few coupons, people had to choose plain, hard-wearing clothes, rather than fashionable, frivolous ones. In any case, the latter were hard to find. Most wartime governments imposed various restrictions limiting the amount of fabric that could be used in the making of a garment and the use of decorative details such as pocket flaps and trouser turn-ups. In Britain this was called the Utility Scheme.

The result was a skimpy look for both sexes. Skirts rose quickly to knee level in 1939 and stayed there until after the end of the war. Men now wore two-piece suits as a rule (the waistcoat being decreed a luxury), with no trouser pleats and no padding in the shoulders.

However, the picture wasn't entirely drab. Manufacturers were allowed to produce a small number of clothes free of restrictions on fabric and style for those who could collect the necessary number of coupons to buy them. Top designers applied their talents to bringing a little style to utility garments. Many women started making their own clothes (often from furnishing fabrics, which were unrationed) thus giving themselves the opportunity to have as many pleats or frills as they wanted.

Below The 'Utility Scheme' during the war did not allow any extra material for frivolous fashion.

Below Women dressed for war, working in an ammunition factory.

Hats were unrationed and remained as pretty as before the war. They were generally small and worn forward on the head, at an angle, and many had veils. More practical headwear, in the form of the snood, was worn by the many wartime female factory workers to keep their hair out of the machinery. This garment had been around for over a hundred years and was a kind of net made of wool or silk, but during the 1930s and 1940s a more glamorous version of it appeared, which was attached to the back of a small hat. Similarly, the headscarf, formerly worn only by peasant women, became popular with all classes. It was often tied up on the head, turban-style.

Working women also took to wearing trousers at about this time; they were practical and helped to keep stocking-less legs warm. And so trousers became an important part of a woman's wardrobe, as they still are today.

Above *This 1930s black straw hat has a straw swallow and veil trimming. Similar styles continued through the war, as hats were unrationed.*

Elegance Returns

With the end of the war came the 'New Look' in fashion. The look may have been 'new' to the post-war world, but in spirit it drew on Edwardian fashions, with their formality, elegance and glorification of the female form.

The 'New Look'

Few fashions have ever had quite the impact of the 'New Look'. The creation of Christian Dior, it burst on the scene in February 1947, nearly two years after the end of the Second World War. Overnight, skimpy skirts and padded shoulders were out; soft curves, nipped-in waists and long skirts, below the calf, were in. Some of the skirts were pencil-slim, but most were extremely full.

Achieving the right feminine shape required the right undergarments. The boned corset made its reappearance to minimize the waist, and padded bras were introduced to provide the necessary fullness where nature had not.

Even coats often followed the figure. Many of them had princess styling, which means that they were fashioned to follow the natural lines of the waist and hips before flaring out below the thighs. Soon, however, the tent-shaped coat become equally popular, if not more so.

Left *The 'New Look' of the late 1940s. This elegant coat is an example of princess styling.*

Right *Padded bras and boned corsets reappeared to achieve the right feminine shape.*

Over the next ten years until his early death, Dior went from strength to strength. Each of his collections was based on a different shape: there was the 'A' line, the 'H' line and the 'Y' line, for example. His business expanded to become a giant fashion empire, manufacturing and selling not only couture and perfumes but also costume jewellery, stockings, men's neckties and ready-to-wear fashions.

The success of the New Look benefited not only Dior; it also brought about the revival of French haute couture. The intricately constructed garments made popular by Dior, with their draping, stiffening, lining and padding, required all the traditional cutting, fitting and finishing techniques of the craft of dressmaking. Only great couturiers could create such fashions, and most of them were to be found in the French capital. The ready-to-wear manufacturers were unable to successfully copy the 'New Look' and for a few years Paris was once again the unchallenged leader of fashion.

Left *This suit was typical of the 'New Look' created by Christian Dior in 1947.*

Below *The French designer Christian Dior making the final adjustments to one of his creations in 1954.*

Christian Dior (1905–1957)

Up until 1947, Christian Dior had not made much of a mark in fashion. Before the war he had merely done some illustrating and sold some sketches to established couture houses. Then, with the backing of a fabric millionaire, he opened his own business. His very first collection, which appeared in 1947, was the spectacularly successful 'New Look'.

Shapes of the 1950s

With femininity and elegance the underlying themes, the 1950s saw a great variety of shapes. The full, long skirts introduced by Dior, however, remained popular throughout the period. Several full, flounced petticoats were worn to hold the skirt out, and for evening wear, a petticoat with a hoop around the hem had a brief run.

The ball gowns of the period showed the great couturiers at their most assured. Many of these gowns had a sculptural quality, being made of firmly woven fabrics such as taffeta and duchesse satin, draped and stiffened in various ways. The strapless bodice was fashionable, along with halter necks and off-the-shoulder necklines.

The cocktail dress was an innovation of this decade. Some cocktail dresses had a short matching jacket or bolero which could be removed for evening wear. In fact, the dress and jacket ensemble, in both daytime and evening versions, remained popular into the 1960s.

Contrasting with the widely popular bouffant line was the sheath skirt or dress. These were very slim (but still ended well below the knee) with a slit or kick-pleat in the back to allow for some ease of movement.

In the later years of the 1950s the form-fitting shape began to be challenged by the 'sack' dress, which hung loosely around the figure, narrowing over the legs. The chemise, which merely skimmed over the figure, was considerably more popular.

Suits of the late 1950s had short jackets that gently curved in at the waist. They often had three-quarter-length sleeves and collars that stood away from the neck. The most important suit of the decade was made by Chanel. Consisting of a simple, straight and usually collarless jacket, trimmed with braid and buttons and a slim skirt, it would be worn with a neat sailor hat, sling-back pumps and a soft blouse with bow-tied neck. It was – and many would say still is – the last word in chic.

Opposite page The skirt of this 1950s summer dress would have been held out by several full petticoats.

Below A 1950s ball gown with a fashionable strapless bodice and long, full skirt.

Another classic from this period was, of course, the bikini. This garment was named after Bikini Atoll in the North Pacific, where, in 1946, the USA conducted a nuclear atom-bomb test. Observers at the time linked the devastating effect of a nuclear blast with the impact made by the bikini, and the comparison stuck. The bikini became 'the' fashionable swimsuit; and despite the occasional crazes for other styles it seems here to stay.

Right *The cocktail dress was an innovation of the 1950s.*

Right The dinner jacket was popular for formal evening wear in the 1950s.

Back to formality

Men's fashion tends to change more slowly than women's. Thus it was several years after the arrival of the 'New Look' that men began to abandon the square-shouldered, baggy-trousered style of the immediate post-war period in favour of a slimmer, more elegant look.

Narrower shoulders, lapels and trousers now came in. The waistcoat returned; and in Britain (still the leader in men's fashions, although Italy was coming to the fore), the bowler hat was revived. Colours were sober: charcoal grey was the preferred shade for business suits on both sides of the Atlantic. The shirt was usually white.

The formality of this look – dubbed 'Edwardian' in Britain – was accompanied by a touch of dandyism. Coats, which were usually black or almost black, in keeping with the fashion for formality, might often be embellished with velvet collars. The cummerbund became fashionable for evening wear, especially in the USA, while in Britain fancy waistcoats enjoyed a vogue.

Below The dandified Edwardian look was exaggerated in Britain by the 'Teddy boys'. Although it started in the 1950s, some people still follow this style today.

This dandified Edwardian look was taken up and exaggerated by the 'Teddy boys'. Their collar-length, elaborately waved and greased hair, complete with sideburns, was popularized in the USA by Elvis Presley and his imitators and fans. Known politely as a 'ducktail' or 'd.a.' haircut (because of the way it was combed at the back), it served as a mild gesture of defiance in the conservative American society which favoured the short back and sides and, for a while, the militaristic-looking crew cut. Another fashion adopted by British Teddy boys, and their small number of European counterparts, was the so-called 'bootlace tie', which had been popularized by its appearance in countless cowboy movies of the era. These would usually accompany a white shirt and a 1950s version of the Edwardian frock coat. On his feet the Teddy boy would wear crêpe-soled shoes, a fashion spawned by the arrival of rock-'n'-roll.

Fashions for the Young

The 1960s saw a revolution in fashion – for the first time in history young people were setting the styles for the older generation.

Below A revolution in fashion started in London in the mid-1960s. The King's Road and Carnaby Street were full of boutiques selling fashions specifically for young people.

The mini skirt

Throughout history, up until the mid-1960s, fashion was designed for the grown woman – the woman in her twenties, thirties or older. Women's styles would then be adapted for teenagers and young girls. The post-war teenager might have fashions of her own for informal wear, such as the sloppy-Joe sweater worn by American schoolgirls, but when she dressed up, she looked very much like her mother.

When the 1960s began, this was still true. Grown-up elegance was the norm, exemplified by Jackie Kennedy, wife of the US President, whose neat little suits and pillbox hats were eagerly adopted by American women.

Then in the mid-1960s came the revolution. It started in London. A new generation of teenagers, born since the war and with money to spend, was beginning to assert its identify with clothes that owed little to parental ideas of good taste. Seemingly overnight, the King's Road and Carnaby Street sprouted dozens of boutiques, all crammed with young fashions and young customers. What they were buying, among other items, was the mini skirt.

Almost instantly the mini skirt became high fashion. André Courrèges gave it French flair in his 1965 collection, and designers around the world leaped on to the band-wagon. So did women of all ages and all sizes. They had little choice. In those days there was still a single fashionable look. The only alternatives to the mini were dresses designed specifically for elderly women. Mothers now – for the first time in history – tried to look like their daughters.

Above *The mini skirt was at its briefest in 1967–8. These girls are wearing the house of Dior's 'New Look', commemorating the twentieth anniversary of its founder's 1947 'New Look'.*

Clothes for the space age

Although the mini could be interpreted in feminine ways – in floral printed fabrics, for example – its most fashionable version was 'hard-edge': characterized by stiff, plain fabrics with ultra-simple cut and seaming. Plastic (sometimes transparent) was used for coats and boots. The designs of Pierre Cardin showed the influence of the space exploration programmes undertaken by the USA and the Soviet Union during the 1960s. Many of them consisted of sleeveless tunics worn over skinny-ribbed pullovers and tights (which had taken the place of stockings), boots and visor-type hats. Paco Rabanne took the space age theme even further, with garments made of metal or plastic discs linked by rings.

Lesley Hornby shot to fame as a model in 1966. Her boyish figure set the look for the late 1960s and earned her the nickname Twiggy.

To complement such clothes, hair was straight and preferably cut short in the severely geometrical style introduced by Vidal Sassoon, or longer and teased into a smooth helmet shape. The fashionable face had pale lips and heavily made-up eyes. The English model Twiggy, then still in her teens, with her waif-like features, sleek little head and boyish figure, was the image of the 1960s.

Mary Quant (born 1934)

Born in London, Mary Quant was still in her twenties when the 1960s began. She had studied art at Goldsmiths College in London and in 1955 – along with her husband, Alexander Plunket Green – had opened a fashion boutique in London's King's Road. Frustrated because she couldn't obtain from the manufacturers the kind of young-looking clothes her customers wanted, she began designing them herself. With no previous training in dress design, she learned the basics in a hurry. Her first efforts were produced by a few dressmakers working in her own bedsitter. Despite the conditions under which they were conceived and made, these perky little dresses sold instantly, and in 1963 she and her husband went into mass production, launching the line called Ginger Group. Since then, the Quant empire has grown to include cosmetics, tights, costume jewellery, sunglassses, men's neckties and even bed linen.

Whether or not Mary Quant actually originated the mini skirt is uncertain, but she certainly did more than anyone else to satisfy the desire of the young for fashions of their own.

Top right Plastic was often used for coats and boots in the 1960s and reflected the influence of the space exploration programmes.

Bottom right Mary Quant led the way in producing inexpensive clothes and cosmetics for young women in the 1960s.

Bright young men

For men, as well as women, the mid-1960s brought some startling changes in fashion. After more than a hundred years of mainly neutral shades, men's clothing burst into colour. Shirts were now coloured – not only blue, but green, yellow, mauve and even pink. Some were patterned. Ties were even more colourful, often printed in paisley or vivid patterns showing the influence of Op Art, Pop Art and mind-expanding drugs. Even suits were more colourful; one London designer produced a suit made of red, orange and gold striped upholstery fabric.

The general trend in the late 1960s was towards a wider line: broad lapels, flared trousers and the 'kipper' necktie, measuring as much as 16cm at its widest point. Contrasting with this trend was a new version of the slim line. Pierre Cardin designed a collarless jacket, which became popular once it was worn by the Beatles (whose distinctive haircuts were instantly adopted by every stylish man under thirty). The Beatles also helped to popularize the fashion of wearing a polo-necked sweater, rather than a shirt and tie, with a suit.

Right *After a century of dull shades men's fashions suddenly burst into colour in the mid-1960s.*

Below *The Beatles in the 1960s. Ringo (right) is wearing a single-breasted, collarless jacket designed by Pierre Cardin.*

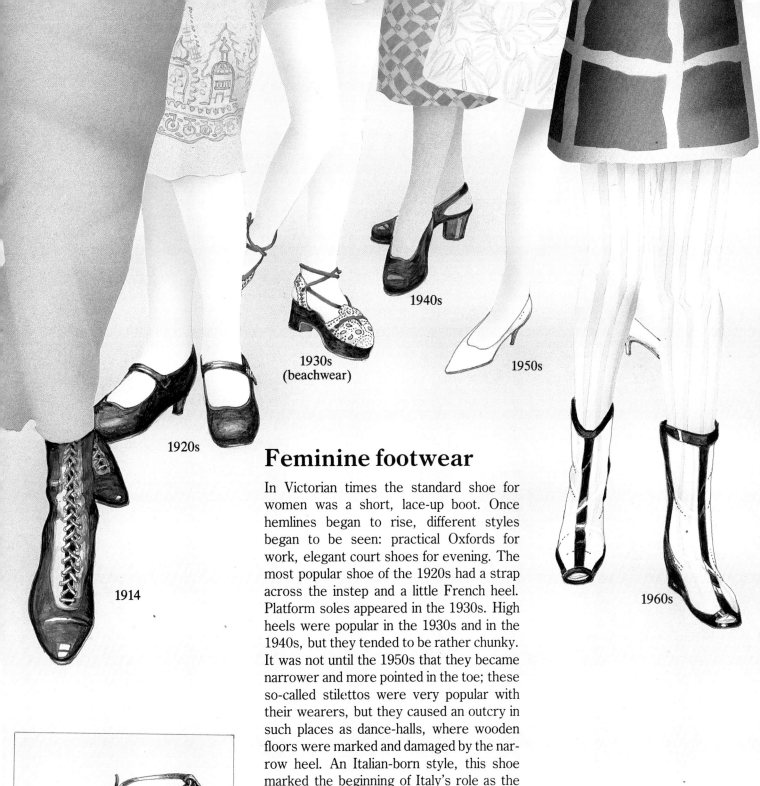

1940s

1930s
(beachwear)

1950s

1920s

1914

1960s

Feminine footwear

In Victorian times the standard shoe for women was a short, lace-up boot. Once hemlines began to rise, different styles began to be seen: practical Oxfords for work, elegant court shoes for evening. The most popular shoe of the 1920s had a strap across the instep and a little French heel. Platform soles appeared in the 1930s. High heels were popular in the 1930s and in the 1940s, but they tended to be rather chunky. It was not until the 1950s that they became narrower and more pointed in the toe; these so-called stilettos were very popular with their wearers, but they caused an outcry in such places as dance-halls, where wooden floors were marked and damaged by the narrow heel. An Italian-born style, this shoe marked the beginning of Italy's role as the world leader in women's shoe fashions. Boots began to be stylish, instead of merely practical, in the 1960s. Since then, they have taken many forms, from ankle to thigh-high, but look as if they are here to stay. Recently the rounded and squared toes of the late 1960s and 1970s have given way to a revival of the pointed toe, while sandals in every colour of the rainbow brighten the shop windows in summer.

1980s

1970–1990

Fashion Free-For-All

The 1970s and 1980s have been characterized by an unprecedented freedom of expression in fashion.

New fashion attitudes

The fashion revolution of the 1960s was characterized by one significant trait: overnight, everyone looked – or tried to look – young. The revolution of the 1970s and 1980s is far more complex. It involves a whole new attitude to fashion. No longer is there a single 'look'. Instead, there is a whole range of different looks at any one time. These looks come and go, as in the past, and some colours will be 'in' and seen in every shop window, while others will be 'out' and impossible to find. But there is a lot more freedom of choice. The young and old of both sexes can select the look they like, or they can put together their own individual look. Indeed, many recent fashions have built their popularity on the very fact that they are not widely followed; they seem to gain extra prestige by not being 'what everyone else is wearing'.

Also, there is no longer a single fashion 'capital'. Paris still ranks first, but Milan, New York and London are nearly as important, and many of the most original talents working in Paris today are Japanese.

Right This show confirms that Paris is still the fashion capital of the world.

Below The Japanese fashion designer Kenzo.

The last two decades have also seen the decline of haute couture. The major couturiers realized in the 1970s that the expanding market was for high-quality ready-to-wear, or, as the French call it, prêt-à-porter. Led by Yves Saint Laurent, the most influential designer of the past twenty years, they have gradually reduced or discontinued their haute couture lines. Today the fashion news comes from the twice-yearly showings of the new ready-to-wear collections, but couture still has a following among the rich. As haute couture has declined and mass-production flourished, the manufacturing of fashionable clothes has to a large extent relocated itself. While cities such as Paris, New York and London have retained their pre-eminence in terms of design, more and more fashion clothes are being made thousands of kilometres away in such places as the Far East, India and parts of southern Europe, among others. Cheaper labour and growing expertise in these areas have led many of the best-known names in western fashion to relocate their production departments overseas.

Above A model on the catwalk at one of the twice-yearly showings of the ready-to-wear collections in Paris.

Looks of the 1970s

The saying 'What goes up must come down' applies in fashion as elsewhere, and around 1970, when the possibilities of the mini skirt had seemingly been exhausted, hemlines plunged. (The fashion industry, after all, depends for its livelihood on making last year's garments look old-fashioned.) The below-the-calf midi skirt enjoyed brief popularity in the early 1970s; the ankle-length maxi came and went in a hurry. However the long skirt did catch on in a more romantic form, especially in Britain. Inspired partly by the 'hippies' or 'flower children', the look was innocent and old-fashioned. It was mainly the creation of Laura Ashley, and garments were made in her own still-fashionable flower-sprigged cotton fabrics. Long frilled dresses and pinafores, often topped with a crocheted shawl, were worn by the young even during the daytime. Peasant-style smocks were worn over long skirts or trousers. The long skirt and contrasting blouse remained fashionable evening wear for women of all ages until the late 1970s.

Below *Devotees of the mini skirt did not like the fashion for midi skirts in the early 1970s.*

Above *A mother and daughter are both dressed in the long, ethnic look.*

Left *Romantic, flowing robes were popular during the early 1970s.*

The trouser suit and the jumpsuit, introduced in the 1960s, carried on into the 1970s. The former was especially popular for town wear and travel. For the very young and slim there was also the successor to the mini, hot pants – as short-lived as they were short.

The 'ethnic look' enjoyed a run of several years in the early 1970s. Fabrics inspired by those of India (or actually woven there), South America, the Middle East and other exotic places came into fashion and were used in the creation of flowing, layered styles. The caftan was one of the most common garments made from fabrics of this sort. This long, loose garment, inspired by robes traditionally worn in parts of Asia, was worn by hippies – male and female – in public as well as in private, along with sandals and strands of beads. It was adopted by more conventional middle class women for lounging and entertaining.

Unisex

The Women's Movement, the fitness craze and assorted other social trends have all contributed to the fashion known as unisex. Styles that can be worn by men or women are now a familiar part of the fashion landscape.

The first unisex garment was designed back in 1850 by a gold prospector. He needed some trousers that would withstand a lot of wear, so he made some for himself out of blue denim, with pockets secured by copper rivets. His name was Levi Strauss.

Since then levis, or jeans, have been worn by cowboys, lumberjacks and other working men. In the 1940s and 1950s jeans became popular among American teenage girls, but only for casual wear. It was only in the 1970s that they became the world's most fashionable garment – worn by both sexes and all ages, not only to the office but to the theatre. Enterprising designers produced their own versions, bearing their name or initials, for high prices, but these prestige garments were not truly fashionable until they had been well-faded and shrunk to the desired skin-tight fit.

Other popular unisex fashions include the tracksuit (worn with bright-coloured cushioned training shoes or sneakers), the T-shirt, the sweatshirt, baggy pullovers and leather jackets.

Related to the unisex trend is the recent vogue for masculine-looking clothes for women. In an effort to make their male colleagues take them more seriously, some American women executives have taken to wearing 'power suits' – severely tailored outfits resembling a man's suit, except for the skirt. Much more widespread was the mid-1980s fashion for big shoulder pads in virtually all women's garments, including soft blouses.

Below Denim jeans and shirt make up the unisex look of the 1980s.

Left *T-shirts are one of the most popular unisex fashions of the 1980s.*

Below left *Some women have started wearing 'power suits' so that they will be taken more seriously in business.*

Surrounded by aggressive-looking women, men have responded by wearing jackets with even bigger shoulder pads, which make them look like a cross between a Chicago gangster of the 1920s and the Incredible Hulk.

Street fashion

The great influence that young people began to exert over fashion in the 1960s is as strong as ever in the 1980s. Street fashion – a look put together by young people from slightly modified finished clothes, often in imitation of a favourite pop group – will now turn up a year or two later, refined and made in expensive materials, in the collections of top designers. Punk, the sensation of the late 1970s, started on the streets of London, among fans of the notorious Sex Pistols. The torn, safety-pinned jackets, shirts and trousers sported by punks were essentially designed by themselves, but it wasn't long before the garish colours and spiky hairdos found their way into the glossy fashion magazines. Britain's Zandra Rhodes produced a typically luxurious 'Punk Chic' collection featuring, among other details, gold safety pins.

Street fashion has never been as popular in other countries as it is in Britain. Yet whatever the current look among British teenagers – cowboy, garage mechanic or Samurai warrior – traces of it are certain to crop up in smart boutiques from Stockholm to Sydney.

Above The British designer Zandra Rhodes modelling one of her 'Punk Chic' collection.

Right Street fashion – first popularized in the 1970s by skinheads.

The superior sweater

Some of the most exciting fashions of the 1980s have been created in knitwear. Knitting itself, of course, has been around for centuries, but up until the twentieth century sweaters were worn mainly by peasants and fishermen. Chanel adapted the cardigan for women's fashions in the 1920s, while men donned slipovers and pullovers worked in Fair Isle and Argyll patterns.

Elegant embroidered and beaded cardigans enjoyed a vogue, especially in the USA, during the 1950s. This was also the era of the 'sweater girl', who showed off her curves in tight-fitting ribbed pullovers.

Even so, the sweater generally had a 'practical but boring' image until the 1970s. Then, thanks to innovators such as the Italian design team Missoni, Britain's Patricia Roberts and, more recently, the American Kaffe Fassett, the sweater has come into its own. With exciting colour patterns and an amazing variety of yarns – including everything from mohair to ribbon and strips of suede – knitwear designers are producing garments of startling and refreshing originality.

Above *The Italian knitwear designers, the Missonis.*

Fashions for the 1980s

The bewildering variety of fashions current today reflects a whole spectrum of attitudes towards dress. Two strong new influences on the international scene are those of the United States and Japan. The American genius is for casual, understated elegance; that of the Japanese designers is for dramatic shapes, often inspired by traditional Japanese costume.

Against the recent trend of making women look like men, there is a growing tendency to go to the opposite extreme, with clothes that are decorative, frivolous and obviously uncomfortable. Turning the pages of a fashion magazine, we find a picture of a model wearing a corset. A return to 1950s glamour, perhaps? Or to Edwardian captivity? Well, yes and no; for this corset is intended to be worn on the outside!

Left The relaxed look of American fashion is illustrated by this outfit designed by Calvin Klein.

Opposite page, right Dramatic shapes and colours by the Japanese designer Jap.

Glossary

Art Deco   A style popular in the decorative arts between the two World Wars which featured angular lines and often harsh colour schemes.

Ascot tie   A cravat with wide square ends, usually fastened with an ornamental stud.

Bouffant   A French word describing a style that is full and puffed-out.

Bowler   A man's felt hat with a rounded crown and small curved brim, named after its designer, a British hatmaker called John Bowler. The hat is called a derby in the USA.

Caftan   (also spelled kaftan) A loose, full-length, long-sleeved tunic, originally worn in the Near East.

Chemise   The French word for shirt, also applied to a loose-fitting dress popular in the late 1950s.

Cloche hat   A woman's hat with a snug-fitting crown and little or no brim (from the French word for bell).

Court shoe   A woman's low-cut shoe, without laces or straps.

Couture   The French word for dressmaking or tailoring; often used to refer to haute couture, the business of producing high-fashion garments to measure for individual customers.

Couturier   A designer of couture fashions; a woman designer is a couturière.

Cravat   A scarf worn by men and tied around the neck.

Cubist painters   An early twentieth-century school of painters who depicted natural objects by means of geometrical planes and forms.

Cummerbund   A pleated sash worn by men with formal dress; also sometimes used in women's fashions.

Empire waistline   A waistline positioned just below the bust; fashionable during the empire of Napoleon I.

Flapper   Word used in the 1920s for a young woman who defied the conventional standards of behaviour.

Godet   French word for small gore (a small inserted piece of material), used to provide extra flare in a skirt or sleeve.

Harem trousers   Loose trousers for women, gathered at the ankle, resembling those worn in harems.

Hippie   A person (especially during the 1960s) whose behaviour and appearance implied a rejection of conventional values.

Hobble skirt   A narrow skirt fashionable just before the First World War.

Hot pants   Very brief skin-tight shorts, worn by young women.

Jumpsuit   A one-piece garment consisting of a shirt or bodice and trousers.

Kipper necktie   A very wide necktie popular in the 1960s and 1970s.

Knickerbockers   Baggy, below-the-knee trousers; named after the early Dutch settlers of New York, who wore similar garments.

Lounge suit   A man's business suit; introduced in the late 1800s and standard day wear today.

Maxi   An ankle-length skirt briefly fashionable in the 1970s.

Midi   A mid-calf-length skirt fashionable in the 1970s.

Op Art   A style of art popular in the 1960s which featured striking – often dizzying – optical effects.

Oxford   A type of low-heeled lace-up shoe.

Paisley   An intricately-patterned fabric, characterized by swirling shapes, first used for shawls made in Paisley, Scotland.

Pillbox hat   A woman's small, flat-topped, brimless hat.

Plus-fours   A slightly longer version of knickerbockers.

Pop Art   A style of art popular in the 1960s which imitated mass-produced images such as tin can labels and comic strips.

Princess styling   A term applied to a woman's garment in which there is no waistline and which is cut and seamed to fit the bodice closely and flare out below the waist.

Ready-to-wear   Clothing produced by factory methods for a mass market.

Sailor hat   A woman's hat with a squared crown and a curved-back brim; also called a Breton hat.

Samurai warrior   A warrior of feudal Japan.

Shingle haircut   A woman's short-cropped hair-style popular in the 1920s.

Stiletto heel   A narrow high heel, tapering to a point; named after the small dagger it resembles.

Tracksuit   A one-piece trouser suit worn for exercising.

Tuxedo   An American term for a dinner jacket, or for the complete outfit including it; named after the country club in Tuxedo Park, New York, where it became popular.

Vest   The British word for an undershirt; the American and Australian word for a waistcoat.

Further Reading

Byrde, Penelope, **A Visual History of Costume: the Twentieth Century** (Batsford 1986).

Byrde, Penelope, **The Male Image – Men's Fashion in Britain 1300–1970** (Batsford 1979).

Carter, Ernestine, **20th Century Fashion, A Scrapbook – 1900 to Today** (Eyre Methuen 1975).

Ewing, Elizabeth, **History of 20th Century Fashion** (Batsford 1986).

Laver, James, **Costume and Fashion, a Concise History** (Thames and Hudson 1982).

McDowell, Colin, **McDowell's Directory of Twentieth Century Fashion** (Frederick Muller 1984).

Rothstein, Natalie (Ed.), **Four Hundred Years of Fashion** (Victoria and Albert Museum/ Collins 1984).

Picture acknowledgements
The illustrations in this book were supplied by: Barnaby's Picture Library 5 (right), 15, 17, 18 (left), 19 (above), 20 (left), 23, 24 (left), 25 (left), 27 (left), 30, 34 (left), 37; The Bridgeman Art Library 5 (main), 10 (both), 14 (left), 18 (right), 20 (right); Camera Press 6 (Bassano), 21; ET Archives 9, 11 (right), Charles Harford 44 (left), The Mansell Collection 4, 5 (inset); Syndication International 8 (both), 16 (right), 24 (right), 25 (right), 26, 27 (right), 28 (left), 31, 33 (below), 40, 41 (below); TOPHAM Title page, 7 (left), 11 (left), 12 (left), 13 (both), 14 (right), 16 (left), 19 (below), 22 (right), 28 (right), 29, 32, 33 (above), 34 (right), 36 (both), 38, 39 (both), 41 (above), 42 (both), 43, 44 (right), 45; Malcolm S. Walker 35. The remaining pictures are from the Wayland Picture Library.

Index